The Sounds of Christmas

by Eugene Butler

Please visit our website:
www.FredBockMusicCompany.com

A MIDNIGHT CLEAR

RICHARD S. WILLIS
Arranged by EUGENE BUTLER

JOY!

Arranged by
EUGENE BUTLER

CHRISTMAS SYMBOLS

Arranged by
EUGENE BUTLER

Relaxed, not too fast (♩ = ca. 100)

"The Holly and the Ivy" (Trad. English Carol)

GOD REST YE MERRY, GENTLEMEN

Traditional English Carol
Arranged by EUGENE BUTLER

ANGELS WE HAVE HEARD ON HIGH

Traditional French Carol
Arranged by EUGENE BUTLER

WHAT CHILD IS THIS?

English Folk Melody
Arranged by EUGENE BUTLER

YULETIDE MEDLEY

Arranged by
EUGENE BUTLER

"O Leave Your Sheep"
(Trad. French Carol)

"Lo! How a Rose E'er Blooming"
(Trad. German Carol)

"Good Christian Men, Rejoice" (Trad. German Melody)

A DICKENS CHRISTMAS

Arranged by
EUGENE BUTLER

"Gloucestershire Wassail"
(Traditional English Carol)

"The Boar's Head Carol"
(Trad. English Melody)

"Here We Come A-Wassailing"
(Traditional English Carol)

Do you have these keyboard books from Fred Bock Music Company?

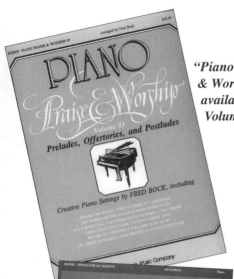

"Piano Praise & Worship" available in Volumes 1–3

"Bock's Best" series is available in Volumes 1–5

Fred Bock's classic arrangements now available for the intermediate pianist

A wonderful book from Jan Sanborn

"Fred Bock Piano Favorites" available in four versions…
–of Bill & Gloria Gaither
–for Christmas
–for Weddings
–for Easter

𝆑𝄐 Fred Bock Music Company

EXCLUSIVELY DISTRIBUTED BY
HAL•LEONARD®

"Bock to Bock" organ/piano duet series is available in Volumes 1–5

"The Organ Music of Fred Bock" is available in Volumes 1–2

Two special memorial collections in tribute to Fred Bock

"Worship Hymns for Organ" is available in Volumes 1–2